Bouquet of Color

by Naoko Ikeda

T0061485

ISBN 978-1-5400-2560-9

WILLIS MUSIC

EXCLUSIVELY DISTRIBUTED BY

HAL•LEONARD®

© 2019 by The Willis Music Co.
International Copyright Secured   All Rights Reserved

For all works contained herein:
Unauthorized copying, arranging, adapting, recording, Internet posting, public performance,
or other distribution of the music in this publication is an infringement of copyright.
Infringers are liable under the law.

Visit Hal Leonard Online at
www.halleonard.com

Contact us:
Hal Leonard
7777 West Bluemound Road
Milwaukee, WI 53213
Email: info@halleonard.com

In Europe, contact:
Hal Leonard Europe Limited
42 Wigmore Street
Marylebone, London, W1U 2RN
Email: info@halleonardeurope.com

In Australia, contact:
Hal Leonard Australia Pty. Ltd.
4 Lentara Court
Cheltenham, Victoria, 3192 Australia
Email: info@halleonard.com.au

Preface

My memories of flowers are happy. There was an abundance of wildflowers on the roadside where I used to walk as a schoolgirl, and flowers were always blooming on the hill I used to play on with friends. The leading characters of this collection are those flowers.

Flowers mean different things in cultures all over the world, but I have included what they mean to me in the notes that follow. I hope they will guide you as you play.

Whenever you find your favorite flowers, make a colorful bouquet of your very own!

Naoko Ikeda

Contents

Notes on the Pieces

Through a Flower Field

It's a bright, sunny day, and you are in the window seat of a train. There are mountains in the distance, but the tracks run through astonishing beds of swaying flower fields, as far as the eye can see. The left hand plays a cheerful staccato in duple time, helping to propel the train forward.

Four-Leaf Clover

Signifies good luck.

Under a blue sky, your mission is to find one lucky clover on a hill covered with soft green. The clover is a flowering plant that can bloom with tiny red, purple, white, or yellow petals. Gently play the staccatos in the middle section: they are sounds of happiness knocking on the door to your heart.

Lily of the Valley

Signifies the sweet return of happiness.

I live on a northern island, and here the lily of the valley symbolizes the arrival of spring. Bring out the bass melody in measure 35.

Snowdrops

Signifies hope and consolation.

Imagine falling snow that transforms to flower petals. There is anticipation that spring will come very soon. Although the piece is brief, the melodies in both hands should move and speak to each other.

Freesias

Signifies friendship and trust.

Start the piece as if you are talking or writing to your best friend who lives far away. The middle section of the piece is a dialogue; use the rests to adjust your hand position.

Irises

Signifies faith and friendship.

A reply to the letter in "Freesias," this relaxed piece is about friendship. The melody should be played elegantly.

Sunflowers

Signifies adoration.

In Peru, sunflowers are a symbol of the Sun God. Think of a flower field where tiny suns (the D Major chords) bloom, and play in a lively manner. The changing meter to A Major reveals the sparkling sun peeking adorably out of a cloud.

Asters

Signifies delicacy and gracefulness.

In Japan, these flowers imply a longing for a distant beloved. Sing while creating a soft, clear sound.

Labyrinth of Blue Roses

Signifies mystery and attaining the impossible.

Mysterious miracles are happening in a syncopated labyrinth of unusual blue roses. The first half of the piece requires speed and boldness. Play expressively. The single chord at the end represents a light that leads out of the labyrinth.

Bouquet

The final piece in this collection is a duet. In this piece, the bouquet symbolizes a hopeful joy. At the start, imagine the bouquet being thrown up to the sky. It travels in the shape of a parabola back down to earth (the Secondo merges with the Primo). Measure 24 should sound like a full organ.

Through a Flower Field

Naoko Ikeda

Allegretto con spirito

© 2018 by The Willis Music Co.
International Copyright Secured   All Rights Reserved

Four-Leaf Clover

Naoko Ikeda

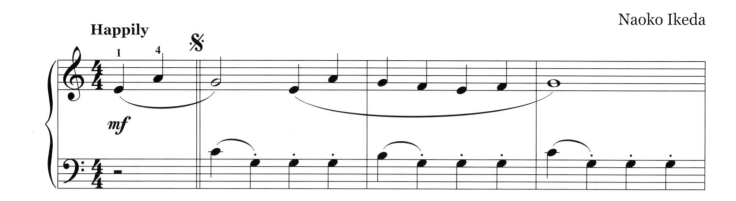

© 2018 by The Willis Music Co.
International Copyright Secured   All Rights Reserved

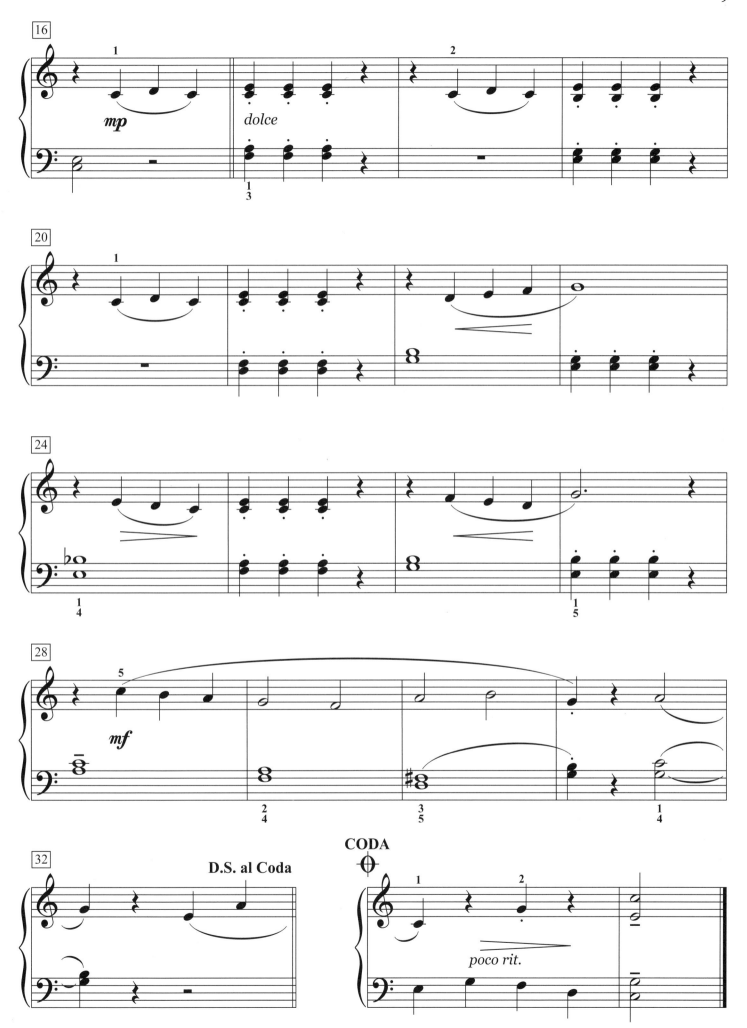

Lily of the Valley

Naoko Ikeda

© 2019 by The Willis Music Co.
International Copyright Secured   All Rights Reserved

Snowdrops

for Ayami Nakagawa

Naoko Ikeda

Andantino cantabile

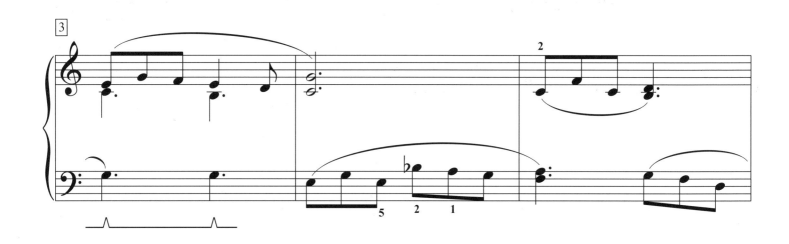

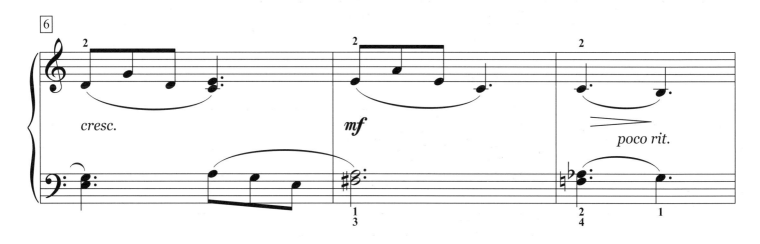

© 2018 by The Willis Music Co.
International Copyright Secured   All Rights Reserved

Freesias

Naoko Ikeda

© 2018 by The Willis Music Co.
International Copyright Secured   All Rights Reserved

Irises

for Nanako Fujita

Naoko Ikeda

© 2018 by The Willis Music Co.
International Copyright Secured   All Rights Reserved

Sunflowers

Naoko Ikeda

© 2018 by The Willis Music Co.
International Copyright Secured   All Rights Reserved

Asters

for Yuri Sato

Naoko Ikeda

© 2018 by The Willis Music Co.
International Copyright Secured   All Rights Reserved

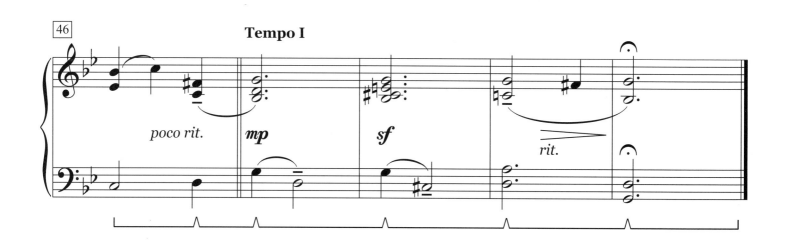

Labyrinth of Blue Roses

Naoko Ikeda

Allegro con energia

© 2018 by The Willis Music Co.
International Copyright Secured   All Rights Reserved

Bouquet

for Yūko and Shigeno

SECONDO

Naoko Ikeda

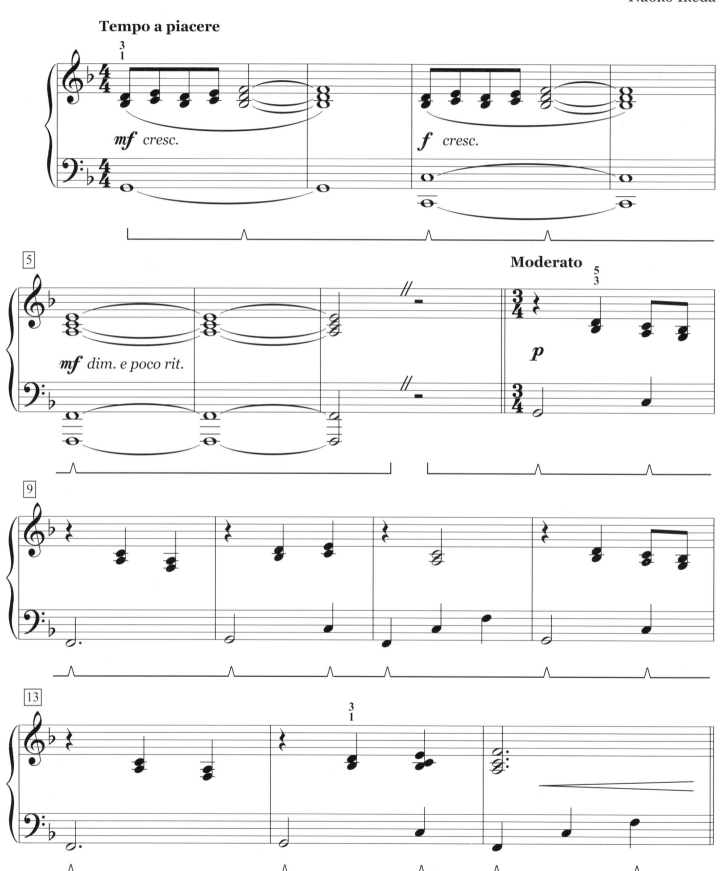

© 2007 by The Willis Music Co.
International Copyright Secured   All Rights Reserved

Bouquet

for Yūko and Shigeno

PRIMO

Naoko Ikeda

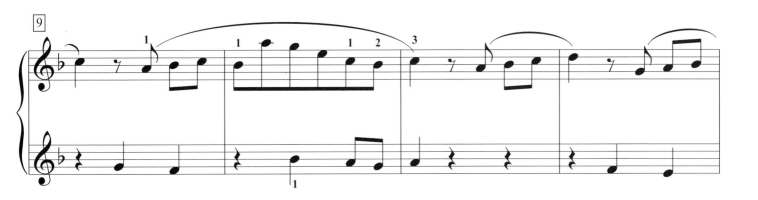

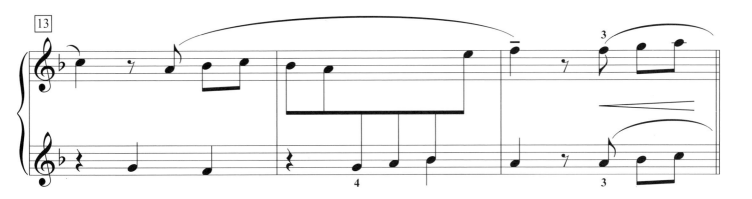

© 2007 by The Willis Music Co.
International Copyright Secured   All Rights Reserved

SECONDO

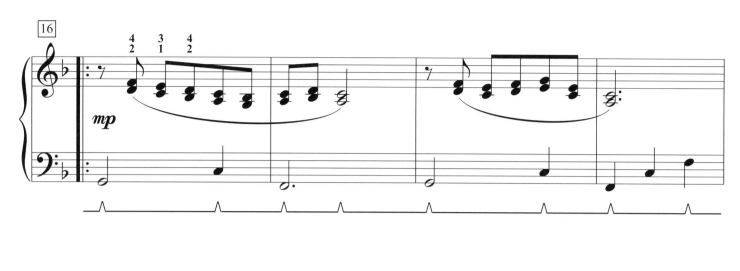

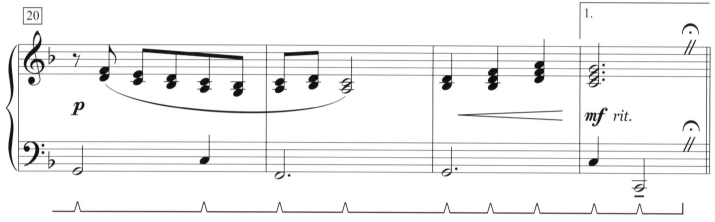

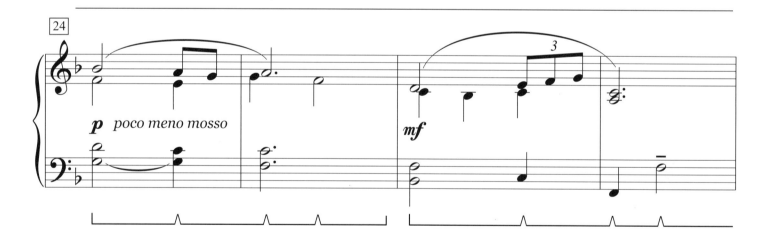

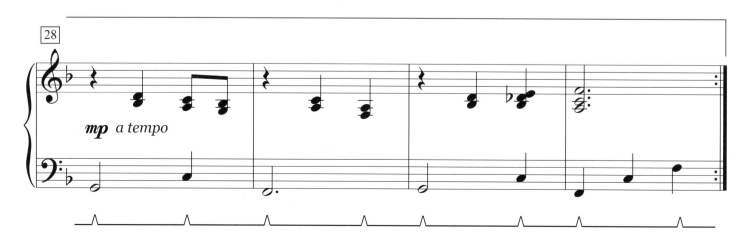

PRIMO

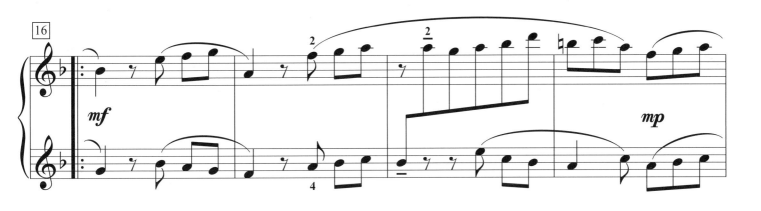

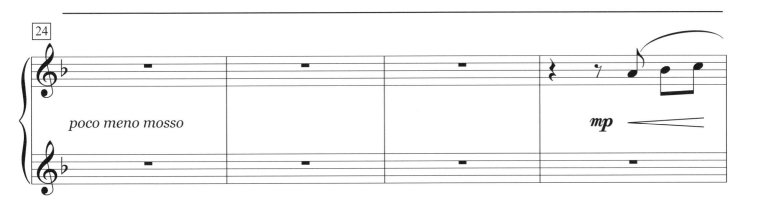

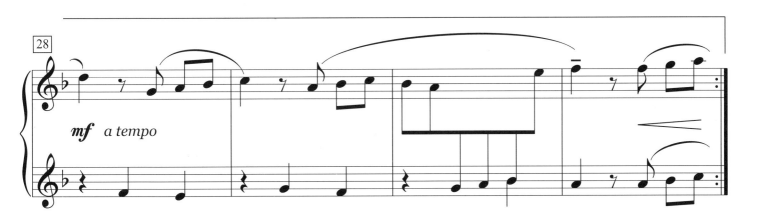

SECONDO

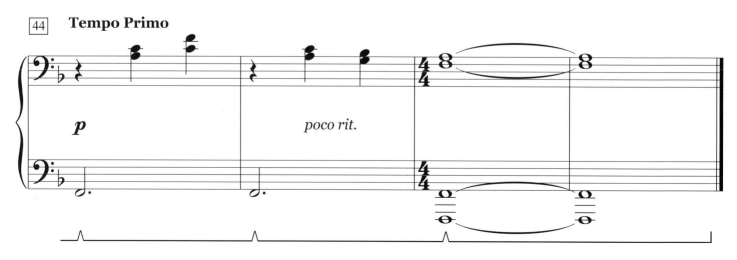

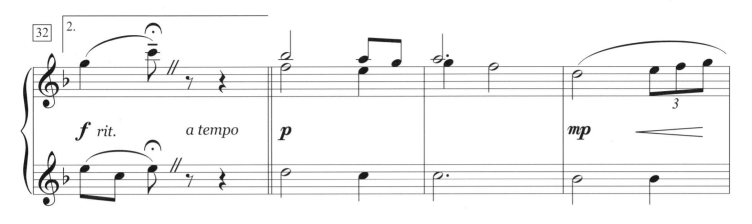

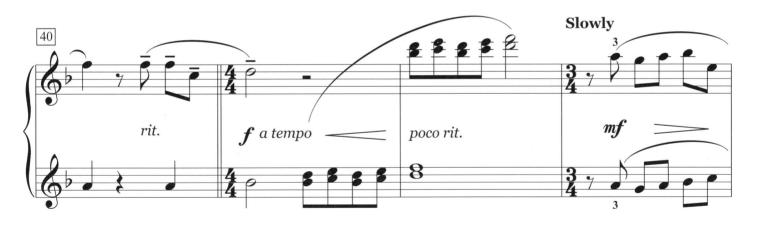

Also by Naoko Ikeda

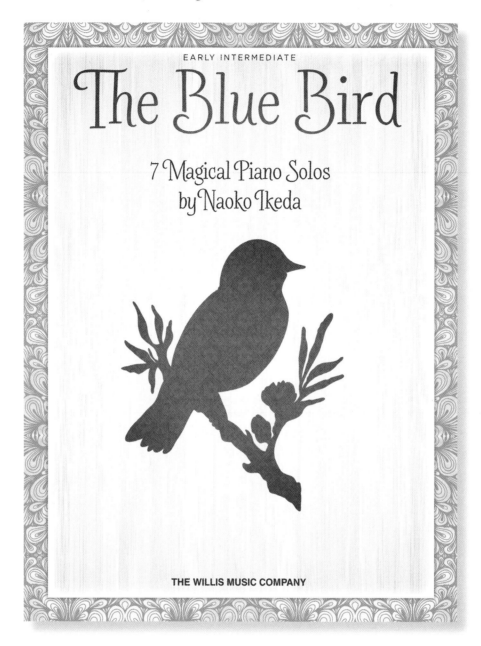

EARLY INTERMEDIATE

The Blue Bird

7 Magical Piano Solos
by Naoko Ikeda

THE WILLIS MUSIC COMPANY

The Blue Bird. An enchanting suite of piano solos inspired by the Maurice Maeterlinck play. Each brief piece captures an emotion, from delight to foreboding, happiness to nostalgia, transporting performer into Naoko's magical musical universe. Titles: Happiness (Prologue) • The Magic Forest • Mysterious Wind • Song of the Blue Bird • The White Rabbit • Dark Blue Night • Happiness (Epilogue). Level: Early Intermediate. **(HL00274262)**